OF MICE AND MEN

by
John Steinbeck

Teacher Guide

Written by
James H Duncan

Note

The 1993 Penguin Books paperback edition of the novel, © 1937 by John Steinbeck and renewed 1965, was used to prepare this guide. The page references may differ in other editions. Novel ISBN: 978-0-14-017739-8

Please note: Parts of this novel deal with sensitive, mature issues. Please assess the appropriateness of this novel for the age level and maturity of your students prior to reading and discussing it with them.

ISBN 978-1-56137-187-7

To order, contact your local school supply store, or—

Novel Units, Inc.
P.O. Box 97
Bulverde, TX 78163-0097

Web site: novelunits.com

Table of Contents

Skills and Strategies

Critical Thinking
Analyzing, inference, research, opinions, prediction

Comprehension
Plot development, compare/contrast, cause/effect

Literary Elements
Foreshadowing, symbolism, conflict, foils, static/dynamic characters, theme

Vocabulary
Definitions, application, synonyms/antonyms

Writing
Essay, poetry, review, journal, letter, synopsis, eulogy

Across the Curriculum
Literature—book review, author interview, John Steinbeck's short stories; History—The Great Depression, migrant workers; Art—cover art, photography, painting, collage; Drama—plays, films

Genre: fiction

Setting: California, near Soledad

Point of View: third-person

Themes: friendship, love, poverty, jealousy, secrecy, loyalty, obedience, mercy, hope, Depression-Era survival, rising above one's circumstances

Conflict: person vs. society, person vs. self, person vs. person

Style: direct narrative in novella form (shorter than a novel, longer than a short story); The descriptive setting details and colloquial dialogue are typical of Steinbeck's style.

Tone: sympathetic, apprehensive, hopeful, forlorn

Date of First Publication: 1937

Summary

George and Lennie are transient workers starting a new job on a ranch near Soledad, California. George is small, wary, and the more intelligent of the two; Lennie is large, strong, and has the mind of a child. They hope the money from this next job will enable them to purchase their own land, start a farm, and raise rabbits for Lennie to tend. Lennie's unwitting desire to touch pretty things has gotten them into trouble before, and George cautions Lennie that if anything bad happens at the new job, he is to hide in the brush beside the river. Once at the ranch, George tries to keep Lennie from talking as much as possible. Curley, the boss's son, is antagonistic and fiercely jealous of any man speaking to his wife, who often hovers around the workers when Curley isn't around. One day, Curley's wife corners Lennie in a barn and convinces the powerful man to touch her hair. When she insists that he let go, Lennie panics and holds on tightly to her hair. Curley's wife screams, and Lennie tries to silence her, accidentally breaking her neck. George, determined to protect Lennie, finds Lennie by the river and begins to repeat the story of their dream farm. As Lennie is daydreaming about tending the rabbits, George shoots him in the back of the head. Distraught, George leaves with the other workers.

About the Author

John Steinbeck was born in Salinas, California in 1902, and many of his novels and short stories take place near this area. He attended Stanford University but never graduated, choosing instead to focus on his writing career. He moved to New York City for a brief period before returning to California. Steinbeck's breakthrough novel, *Tortilla Flat* (1935), takes place in Monterey, a seaside town near Salinas. Thus began Steinbeck's lifelong use of proud yet humble, poverty-stricken characters that make up much of the California working class. Minorities and themes of injustice and class discrimination also play a large role in many of his socially aware works. Notable other novels include *In Dubious Battle* (1936), *Of Mice and Men* (1937), *The Grapes of Wrath* (1939), *Cannery Row* (1945), *The Pearl* (1947), and *East of Eden* (1952). Although Steinbeck won The National Book Award, The Pulitzer Prize for Fiction, and The Nobel Prize for Literature, his books are among the most frequently challenged of the 21st century, mostly due to mature themes and vulgar language. *The Grapes of Wrath* continues to be one of the most challenged books in schools and libraries. Steinbeck is often ranked among the most beloved, controversial, and influential writers of all time, and many of his books are required reading in high schools across the nation. John Steinbeck died in New York City in 1968.

Characters

George Milton: migrant worker; slight man with dark hair and dark eyes; quick thinker; distrustful of others and wary of their reaction to Lennie; tired of caring for Lennie but understands that Lennie has no one else; dreams of owning a farm where he and Lennie can escape from their troubles

Lennie Small: migrant worker; large, powerful man with the mind of a child; unable to care for himself and easily duped by others; terrified by confrontation; obsessed with George's story about their future farm; kindhearted; loves soft things (mice, rabbits, puppies, clothing, hair, etc.), although his compulsion to pet them often gets him and George into trouble

Candy: old man with only one hand; works on the ranch but fears he will be fired soon because of his handicap; learns of George and Lennie's dream farm and agrees to help finance it if he can join them

Slim: tall man who runs a team on the ranch; hard-working, fair, skilled, and well-liked by the other workers; the unofficial leader of the ranch hands; No one knows just what Slim is capable of doing in a fight.

Crooks: black man who lives in the barn and tends to the animals; has a crooked spine; plays horseshoes with the other workers but is generally prohibited from spending time with them because of his race; learns of George and Lennie's dream farm and initially wishes to join them

Carlson: burly man who can be aggressive at times; generally friendly but also selfish; convinces Candy to let him kill his [Candy's] old dog to put it out of its misery; keeps a pistol under his bed

Whit: young ranch hand; likes visiting the brothel in town; reads pulp novels

Curley: ranch owner's son; former boxer; short, volatile man who picks fights with bigger men, including Lennie; always suspicious that other men are trying to sleep with his wife; disliked by almost everyone on the ranch

Curley's wife: attractive young woman; wanders the ranch looking for Curley, although she ultimately tries to avoid him; flirts with any man she encounters; entices Lennie to touch her hair and dies when he accidentally breaks her neck

the boss: owns the ranch; suspicious of George and Lennie

It is important to note the mature subject matter in *Of Mice and Men*. The novel contains numerous instances of profanity and offensive (slang) terminology, as well as scenes of violence (Slim drowning the puppies, Carlson shooting Candy's dog, Lennie killing Curley's wife, and George killing Lennie) and a discussion of prostitution. Please carefully consider your particular community and group of students prior to reading and discussing *Of Mice and Men* with your class.

Initiating Activities

Use one or more of the following to introduce the novel.

1. Have students research how the Great Depression affected American workers. (*Surviving the Dustbowl*, a documentary on the PBS Web site, contains videos, audio interviews, photos, and other information about the topic.) Based upon their research, each student should provide up to three themes they think might appear in *Of Mice and Men*. Discuss the possibility and importance of each theme as a class.
2. Ask students to examine the cover of the novel and formulate two predictions about events that will occur in the story. For example, rabbits hiding might be symbolic of threatened innocence. Students should share their predictions with the class.
3. Using the Attribute Webs on page 20 of this guide, have students brainstorm about "loyalty" and "mercy." Discuss any ideas that students have included on both webs.
4. Have students read the author information segment on the first page of the novel. Students should select another of John Steinbeck's works referenced on that page. Have students research their selected title and hypothesize how the themes in it will be similar to themes that may appear in *Of Mice and Men*.
5. Divide the class into four or five groups to play "Word Survival." Using the Glossary on pages 27–28 of this guide, write a vocabulary word on the board and ask each group (one at a time) to supply either a synonym or an antonym for the word. Each group must rely on the groups' collective knowledge to "survive." Groups should continue to supply synonyms or antonyms for the chosen words until one group cannot answer. The group that cannot answer must have a member of their group sit out. Write another vocabulary word to start a new round. The last group with students remaining is the winner.

Pages 1–37

George—a small, agile man—and Lennie—an enormous, simple-minded man—come to a clearing in the brush just before the ranch where they will be working. While resting, the two men discuss the problems they are running from and George describes their dream farm, a place where they can escape from their troubles. Lennie is obsessed with touching soft things—cloth, hair, mice, and the rabbits that await him at the dream farm—and George is concerned about Lennie making trouble at the ranch. George tells Lennie to return to the clearing if anything goes wrong. George and Lennie arrive at the ranch and meet the other workers. The boss is initially suspicious of the two men, especially when George continues to answer questions on Lennie's behalf, and he is disgruntled that they arrived at the end of the week. George and Lennie meet Candy, an aging ranch worker who lost one of his hands in an accident; Curley, the boss's volatile son who immediately instigates a fight with Lennie; Slim, a well-respected man and designated leader of the ranch hands; Curley's wife, an attractive young woman whom George believes will cause trouble for Lennie; and Carlson, a ranch hand who hates Candy's old, smelly dog. While Lennie is excited about the possibility of owning a puppy, George constantly warns him to keep quiet and stay out of trouble.

Vocabulary
recumbent
bindle
brusquely
elaborate
pantomime
imperiously
anguished
morosely
mollified
pugnacious
derogatory
disengage
profound

Discussion Questions

1. Describe George and Lennie, and explain how they complement one another. *(George is the smaller of the two men and is described as "quick, dark of face, with restless eyes and sharp, strong features" [p. 2]. He is slender but strong, appears to be a smart, quick-thinking man, and is clearly the leader of the duo. George is very careful in manner and speech and is always conscious of impending trouble. Lennie is his exact opposite in almost every way. Lennie is "a huge man, shapeless of face, with large, pale eyes, with wide, sloping shoulders" [p. 2]. He doesn't know his own strength and is quite childlike. Lennie seems incapable of taking care of himself and is always unconsciously placing himself or others in danger. Although George and Lennie differ, they make a good team. George leads and is watchful enough for them both, and Lennie's strength makes them valuable to those looking to hire migrant workers. Lennie depends on George for protection and guidance, and George [begrudgingly] relies on Lennie for purpose and companionship.)*
2. In what ways does Lennie demonstrate he is incapable of caring for himself in the first scene? How does George respond to Lennie's behavior? *(Answers will vary. Suggestions: Lennie dunks his entire head into the pool of water to drink, soaking his hat and not noticing that the water is stagnant. This shows he is impulsive and does not think about the consequences of his actions. When George questions him about the dead mouse he's hiding, Lennie insists that he "ain't got nothin'...Honest" [p. 5]. This is a lie that a small child might tell. Other examples, such as Lennie's almost instant forgetfulness and his desire to hear stories repeated are childlike in nature. George remains frustrated with Lennie and must deal with him firmly: throwing away the dead mouse, scolding Lennie, refusing to tell stories, and threatening to go away. George often repeats, "I could get along so easy and so nice if I didn't have you on my tail" [p. 7], a statement born more from frustration than true malice. George dreams about a life without Lennie but is also ashamed of these thoughts. He truly does care for Lennie but feels burdened by the responsibility.)*

3. According to George, how do most ranch workers live and why are he and Lennie different? What do you think about their plan? *(George says that ranch workers are "the loneliest guys in the world. They got no family. They don't belong no place" [p. 13]. Ranch workers travel from job to job, make money, and then spend it right away. George insists to Lennie that they are different because "we got a future. We got somebody to talk to that [cares] about us" [p. 14]. They plan to earn enough money to buy some land and a house where they can work for themselves raising cows, pigs, chickens, and rabbits. Answers will vary. Owning a piece of land was a common dream for migrant workers during the 1930s, although often an unattainable one. However, George's constant retelling of this plan makes Lennie happy and seems to keep the pair optimistic about the future.)*

4. What instructions does George give Lennie regarding meeting the ranch boss the next day, and what can you tell about George from this? *(George tells Lennie to stay quiet and let him [George] do all of the talking. He also tells Lennie that if any trouble should arise, Lennie should return to the clearing by the river and wait for George. He makes Lennie repeat these instructions several times to ensure he remembers them. George's instructions are inspired by Lennie's past transgressions. George knows Lennie's recklessness, and he is worried that trouble will find them again at the ranch. More than just being prepared, George seems to believe that trouble is inevitable.)*

5. Discuss the scene in which George questions Candy about the box of lice powder he finds near their bunks. What might this scene symbolize? *(Answers will vary. The lice powder tells George that there was and may still be lice or some sort of bug infesting the two beds he and Lennie are offered. This indicates the possible poor quality of their living arrangements and is also a symbol of the deeper "scourges" George and Lennie have yet to encounter. Candy sidesteps George's questions about the lice powder, insisting the man that slept there before George and Lennie was ultra-clean and repeating the words, "Tell you what..." [p. 18], as if trying to placate George. This heightens the sense that something is wrong with their new work situation. Steinbeck uses this scene to foreshadow the dangers awaiting Lennie and George on the ranch.)*

6. Why do you think George is so unkind to Lennie at times, such as when he says, "If I was a relative of yours I'd shoot myself" (p. 24)? *(Answers will vary, but students can assume that George has grown increasingly less patient with Lennie for getting them into trouble wherever they go. Lennie rarely remembers George's instructions, and he attracts the ranch boss's watchful eye during the introductions. George lashes out at Lennie, perhaps because Lennie is an easy target. He tells Lennie that he wishes he [Lennie] had been kicked in the head by a horse, and the vicious comment doesn't even register with Lennie. George's cruelty probably stems from both his anger at being stuck with Lennie and his strong desire and frequent inability to protect Lennie. Students should discuss how George's love for Lennie is belied by his cruel treatment of the man.)*

7. Analyze Curley's character. Why do you suppose he behaves the way he does? *(Curley is an extremely volatile man. He is abrupt and demanding of the workers, and he exudes superiority. He is always looking for a fight, particularly with men bigger than him. Upon noticing George and Lennie for the first time, he seems ready to pounce. Answers will vary, but students should note that Curley seems to resent anyone who is larger than he is. As the ranch boss's son, he picks fights with the workers without fear of retaliation. While Curley appears confident, he is most likely the opposite. Antagonizing larger men gives him the advantage if a fight erupts: if he wins he gets bragging rights, and if he loses the larger man is accused of an unfair fight. In each situation Curley gets what he wants, so it makes him even more brazen.)*

8. What does the author mean when he writes that Candy "was reassured. He had drawn a derogatory statement from George. He felt safe now..." (p. 27)? *(Answers will vary. Up to this point, Candy wasn't sure where George and Lennie's loyalties lay. He was careful not to say too much or speak ill about anyone at the ranch, particularly the boss or Curley. After hearing George's critical response to Curley's gloved hand, Candy felt he could trust the man. He began to speak more openly and negatively about Curley and his wife, without fear that George or Lennie might report the conversation.)*

9. Describe your impression of Curley's wife. Why do you suppose she behaves in such a way around the workers? *(Answers will vary, but students will probably note that Curley's wife flirts with the men daily. She is an attractive young woman, and she seems to be aware of her effect on the men. She "[leans] against the door frame so that her body [is] thrown forward," speaks "playfully," and "[twitches] her body" [p. 31] as she stands in the bunkhouse among the men. Curley's wife, while obviously acting inappropriately in her husband's absence, also appears to be a very lonely person married to a man she doesn't love and who feels trapped in a place she doesn't want to be. She uses her physical appearance to gain attention, which students may believe is worthy of sympathy. Students should discuss whether Curley's wife's behavior is rooted in innocent flirtation, malicious intent, or loneliness. Students may note as they read that Curley's wife is always looking for her husband but never seems to find him.)*

10. Analyze Lennie's plea to George following Curley's wife's departure: "I don' like this place, George. This ain't no good place. I wanna get outta here" (p. 32). Do you think George should have heeded Lennie's cries? *(Answers will vary. Discussion should cover Lennie's recognition of impending disaster [which is usually George's role], his fear of a situation he doesn't really comprehend, and the author's use of foreshadowing.)*

11. How is Slim described? How does Slim immediately make George and Lennie feel welcome at the ranch? *(Slim is a tall man who moves with "a majesty only achieved by royalty and master craftsman...the prince of the ranch" [p. 33]. He is considered the authority on all topics among the other workers, who always stop to listen when he speaks. Even Curley's wife adopts a different manner when Slim arrives in the bunkhouse. He is friendly, gentle, and "[invites] confidence without demanding it" [p. 34]. His age is indiscernible and his large, lean hands are delicate and skilled. Slim is portrayed as the epitome of manliness. As much as Lennie and George are opposites, it could be argued that Slim and Curley are opposites—one tall, the other short; one calm, the other quick-tempered; one esteemed with unknown fighting prowess, the other scorned and known as an eager fighter. Slim immediately makes George and Lennie feel welcome by saying he hopes they both join his team because he needs good men to work with. It is a simple but important compliment for George and Lennie.)*

12. In what ways does Slim's statement, "Maybe ever'body in the whole...world is scared of each other" (p. 35), apply to the storyline? *(Answers will vary. Slim observes that Lennie and George are rare because they trust each other and travel together. He believes most people are scared of everyone around them. At first glance, it seems the characters in the novel are scared of one another. The workers are scared of Curley and his wife [insofar as contact with them could get the men fired from the ranch], Candy is scared of saying anything negative in the wrong company, Curley is scared of Lennie [although he conceals this with machismo], George is scared of confrontation between Lennie and anyone else, Lennie is scared of the entire situation [without understanding why], and everyone fears the ranch boss might fire them one day. Slim seems to be the only person at the ranch who is unafraid and easygoing. This ever-present current of fear perpetuates the idea that no place is safe for George and Lennie.)*

13. **Prediction:** If Lennie is allowed to keep a puppy, how will this affect the rest of the story?

Supplementary Activities

1. Research the literary term "foil." Write a brief essay explaining which character(s) from *Of Mice and Men* you think is a "foil," and describe at least three other "foil" characters from literature, movies, or television.
2. Research the history of hobos and migrant workers. Write a brief essay about what life was like for these travelers, and explain how life would be different today for those same types of people.
3. Imagine you are a migrant worker in the 1930s and can only take your most treasured items with you when you travel. Make a list of eight items you couldn't bear to part with. Then, make a list of eight items necessary for your daily survival. Share your lists with the class. Are there any items that appear on both of your lists?
4. Complete a Vocabulary Word Map like the one on page 21 of this guide for six vocabulary words from this section.

Pages 38–65

George and Lennie get along well with the other ranch workers, spending most of their time with Slim and Candy. Slim allows Lennie to care for the puppies, which keeps Lennie both happy and preoccupied. Carlson continues to gripe about Candy's smelly dog, claiming the merciful thing to do would be to kill it. He ultimately convinces Candy to allow him [Carlson] to shoot the dog. Although most of the men agree it is the best thing for the dog, there is an uncomfortable silence in the bunkhouse as the workers await Carlson's return. Whit tells George that Curley's wife has been causing trouble for some of the men, which doesn't surprise George. Whit tries to convince George to join them at a brothel in town, but George declines, insisting that he and Lennie need to save their money. In the absence of the other men, Lennie pleads for George to talk about their dream farm. Candy overhears and begs to join them, as he is looking for a place to settle down and feel valued. He offers to help fund the venture. George and Lennie agree to Candy's request as long as he keeps the plan a secret. Later, Curley antagonizes the men as he searches for his wife, accusing Slim in particular of fooling around with her. He is unable to rile Slim and is soon mocked by the other workers. Curley, believing that Lennie is laughing at him, viciously attacks him. Lennie endures the assault until George orders him to retaliate. Lennie finally grabs Curley's hand and crushes it, breaking all of the bones. Slim protects Lennie by convincing Curley to lie about what happened, and the men take Curley to a doctor.

Discussion Questions

1. What does George confess to Slim about his time with Lennie? How does Slim respond, and why do you think George chooses to confide in Slim? *(George tells Slim how he agreed to take care of Lennie after Lennie's aunt died. George's story becomes more of a confession, and he explains how he used to make fun of Lennie and treat him cruelly because it was easy to do. He even beat up Lennie a few times, and Lennie never defended himself. One day, George wanted to show off in front of a group of men, so he told Lennie to jump in a river. Lennie did and almost drowned, and George felt so guilty that he stopped taking advantage of Lennie's ignorance and naïveté. George tries to explain how hard it has been to live with Lennie, almost as if he's trying to defend his regrettable past behavior. He reveals that at their previous job, Lennie tried to touch a woman's dress. She accused him of rape, and George and Lennie had to escape a lynch mob in the middle of the night.*

Vocabulary
derision receptive nuisance irrigation cultivator deliberate sarcastically subsided reprehensible reverently bemused cowering

Slim listens calmly, and when George finishes, Slim observes that Lennie "ain't mean...I can tell a mean guy a mile off" [p. 42]. Answers will vary. Slim has already been identified as the workers' confidant and the designated leader of the men. George trusts that Slim will keep his secrets, and he probably needs to unburden himself of his feelings about Lennie. Slim "neither encouraged nor discouraged him" [p. 39], and George is confident to continue when he sees Slim's "calm, God-like eyes" [p. 40]. George believes he can trust Slim, and it is helpful for George to share his story.)

2. Analyze Slim's statement to George: "Guy don't need no sense to be a nice fella. Seems to me sometimes it jus' works the other way around. Take a real smart guy and he ain't hardly ever a nice fella" (p. 40). Explain whether you agree or disagree with Slim. *(Answers will vary.)*

3. How does Carlson feel about Candy's dog, and how does Candy respond? What do you think this shows about each man? *(Carlson suggests that Candy is cruel for letting the dog suffer. Carlson states that the dog is old and smelly. He claims not to understand why Candy would want to keep the animal around. Candy is uncomfortable with the discussion and keeps apologizing for his dog. He explains that he's had the dog forever and insists it has been a good, faithful dog. Answers will vary. Some students may feel that Carlson is being practical, although he shows very little understanding or empathy for Candy's feelings or loyalty to the dog. Other students may feel that Carlson is simply taunting Candy, playing on an old man's uncertainties about aging and death. Candy's response shows great sentimentality but also fear. The situation mirrors his fear that his own life is now of little worth because of his age and handicap. Although he fears his dog's death [much like he fears his expulsion from the ranch] and looks to the other workers for affirmation, Candy eventually allows Carlson to shoot the animal.)*

4. Why do you think the men all wait (mostly) silently while Carlson shoots the dog outside? *(Answers will vary, but students should observe that the men agreed with Carlson about what the dog's fate should be. However, they also feel ashamed about not objecting [for Candy's sake] or being more comforting to Candy about the situation. It is obviously a task no one feels good about, and even Carlson doesn't look at Candy when he returns.)*

5. When Whit hears George talking about the temptation and danger surrounding Curley's wife, he invites George to join the men at a brothel in town. What does a night out represent for George, and how does he respond? *(Answers will vary. A night out could be a chance for George to interact with other men of his demeanor and intelligence outside of a work environment. This is not something he has been able to do since taking on the responsibility of caring for Lennie. It also represents a chance for George to be frivolous and self-satisfying, as he previously claimed: "if I was alone...when the end of the month come I could take my fifty bucks and go into town and get whatever I want. Why, I could stay [out] all night" [p. 11]. This is exactly what Whit is offering, but George declines in order to save money for the dream that he shares with Lennie—owning a farm. The night out is his temptation toward selfish pleasure, but he chooses responsibility and loyalty instead.)*

6. Why does George interrogate Lennie so thoroughly when Lennie returns from playing with the puppies in the barn? Do you think George overreacts when it comes to Lennie? Why or why not? *(George is still trying to foresee and prevent problems for himself and Lennie, so he demands to know everything Lennie saw and did in his absence. George wants to know about Slim—where he was, what he was doing, and if Curley's wife was with him. George has already exhibited his disdain for Curley's wife, and he anticipates a fight. George wants Lennie as far away from that as possible so they both stay out of trouble, and he tells Lennie to "keep out of it" [p. 55]. Answers will vary. Students should discuss the responsibilities involved with caring for a person like Lennie—one who is childlike yet an adult, meek yet physically strong, kind yet capable of inflicting harm, and innocent yet an easy scapegoat.)*

7. How does George initially react when he realizes Candy overheard his story about the dream farm? Why do you think he reacts this way? *(After George concludes his story to Lennie, Candy asks him if he knows where such a place is. George immediately becomes defensive, demanding "What's that to you?" and "You couldn't find it in a hundred years" [p. 59]. Answers will vary. George is suspicious of Candy's inquiries and knows the boss will fire them if he finds out about the dream farm because he wants only long-term employees. George also wishes to keep the original plan in which he and Lennie were "gonna do it by [themselves]" [p. 59]. George probably feels like he can better control life with Lennie and prevent trouble if he and Lennie are alone. George may also feel somewhat embarrassed and afraid that Candy will laugh at him and Lennie.)*

8. Why does Candy plead with George to let him join them at their dream farm? What is Candy's greatest fear? What do you think contributes to this fear? *(Candy is convinced that his employment on the ranch is in jeopardy because of his handicap and his age. He knows it's just a matter of time before he's fired, and he desperately wants to feel useful and wanted. Candy's greatest fear is being alone, which is most likely the reason he kept his dog with him, even though the dog was old and dying. His fear is evidenced in his statement to George: "When they can me here I wisht somebody'd shoot me...I won't have no place to go..." [p. 60]. Answers will vary, but students should note that Candy is old and his handicap prevents him from doing much work at the ranch. The other workers, while they feel some pity for the man, keep their distance from Candy and don't involve him in their activities. Candy doesn't have any relatives, cannot get another job due to his handicap, and will most likely have to live in a county institution once he leaves the ranch. All of these factors make Candy fearful and miserable about his future.)*

9. How do the other workers treat Curley when he enters the bunkhouse? Why are they acting this way? *(It is implied that Curley has accused Slim of indiscretions with his wife. Slim is angry about Curley's constant accusations and cautions Curley to leave him alone. The other men are also weary of Curley's wife bothering them and Curley always accusing them of adultery, and so they begin to mock him. Carlson laughs at Curley's attempt to scare Slim and rebuffs Curley's return threat, claiming Curley is "yella as a frog belly" [p. 62]. Even Candy joins in, teasing Curley about his infamous gloved hand. Answers will vary, but students can assume that the men feel comfortable taunting Curley with Slim around. Curley appears to be somewhat afraid of Slim, and the men know that he is unlikely to retaliate as long as Slim is present. They take advantage of the opportunity to express themselves without fear of consequences.)*

10. Why do you think Curley attacks Lennie? How do Lennie and George react? What do you think this proves about Lennie? *(Answers will vary. Curley feels trapped in the bunkhouse while all the other men taunt him. He is furious but unable to do much about it. When he sees Lennie smiling, he jumps at the opportunity to start a fight, knowing a fight with Lennie is the only one he can presently win. Curley's low self-esteem and cowardice cause him to attack Lennie. Students should discuss whether Curley actually believed Lennie was laughing at him or if he just wanted to pick a fight. When Curley attacks Lennie, Lennie tries to get away from him and pleads with George*

to stop Curley. He's too terrified even to defend himself. When George finally shouts, "Get 'im, Lennie... I said get him" [p. 63], Lennie reaches up and grabs Curley's hand, crushing the bones. He doesn't let go until George slaps him in the face and screams at him to stop. Lennie is devastated, saying "You tol' me to, George" and "I didn't wanta hurt him" [p. 64]. Answers will vary, but students should note that Lennie was well-bloodied before he fought back and may have never touched Curley if it weren't for George's urgings. Lennie is a "gentle giant" who is capable of doing much damage but prefers to live peacefully.)

11. What "deal" does Slim make with Curley? How do you suppose Slim so easily convinces Curley to lie about the incident? *(To protect Lennie and George, Slim convinces Curley to tell anyone who asks that he hurt his hand in a machine on the ranch. Just as Slim expected, Curley agrees to do so. Answers will vary. Slim knows that Curley fears shame and humiliation, and if anyone knew that Lennie easily crushed his hand, Curley would be devastated. Curley is known around the ranch for being a fighter, and his disdain for larger men is evident. Slim plays off of Curley's insecurities in order to convince him to lie.)*
12. **Prediction:** How might Curley get revenge on Lennie?

Supplementary Activities

1. Use magazine clippings to create a collage of one of the following scenes from this section: the men waiting uncomfortably in the bunkhouse with Candy, George telling Lennie and Candy about the dream farm, Lennie tending to the puppies in the barn.
2. Complete the Cause/Effect Chart on page 22 of this guide.
3. Complete the Thought Bubble activity on page 23 of this guide.

Pages 66–107

Lennie visits Crooks, the black stable hand. Crooks initially wants Lennie to leave his room, but he soon realizes that Lennie is simple-minded and trustworthy. Crooks poses the idea that George might not come back from town and that Lennie will be left alone. Lennie becomes both angry and frightened, insisting that George will always come back for him. Lennie tells Crooks about the dream farm, but Crooks isn't convinced it is real until Candy arrives and they discuss it more. Crooks is interested and acts pleasant until Curley's wife comes into the barn. Crooks once again becomes agitated and insists that everyone leave. The next day, Lennie is playing with his puppy in the barn when he accidentally kills it. Angry and frightened, he hastily covers the puppy with hay just as Curley's wife enters the barn. She sits and talks to Lennie, eventually convincing him to stroke her hair. Lennie musses her hair, and she gets angry and demands that he let go. Lennie covers her mouth so no one will hear her yelling at him. As he tries to silence her, he shakes her so hard that he breaks her neck. Terrified, Lennie flees the barn. Candy finds Curley's wife's body first and tells only George. When the other men (including Curley) discover the body, they form a search party to find Lennie. George slips away unnoticed and finds Lennie in their hiding place. As George calms Lennie by talking about the dream farm, he shoots Lennie in the back of the head. The other men arrive, and only Slim knows the truth about what George did and why he did it.

Vocabulary
accumulated liniment disarming apprehension scornful crestfallen sniveled skittered retorted belligerently monotonous

Discussion Questions

1. How does Crooks feel about Lennie's intrusion? Do you believe he is justified in feeling this way? *(Crooks is frustrated by Lennie's appearance in his room. Crooks tells Lennie that he has "no right to come in [his] room" [p. 68]. He tries to explain the dynamics of the ranch by telling Lennie, "I ain't wanted in the bunkhouse, and you ain't wanted in my room" [p. 68]. Crooks is an ill-treated outcast among the other workers, and he feels that Lennie is invading his privacy. However, Crooks is also astounded at Lennie's casual and uncomprehending responses to Crooks' comments. Crooks realizes that Lennie is harmless and did not intrude on him purposely. Lennie's curiosity and ignorance show that he isn't prejudiced and doesn't understand the concept of racism. Answers will vary, but most students will agree that Crooks is justified because he is treated so poorly at the ranch. He prefers to be left alone.)*
2. Analyze Crooks' conversation with Lennie regarding George being in town with the other workers. Why do you suppose Crooks behaves this way? *(Crooks presents a hypothetical about George not returning from town. Lennie grows increasingly frightened and agitated as Crooks continues to suggest that George may never return. Crooks seems to delight in upsetting Lennie and making him feel uncertain about George's loyalty to him: Crooks "pressed forward some kind of private victory" and his face "lighted with pleasure in his torture" [p. 71]. Answers will vary. Crooks has most likely never had an opportunity to feel superior to anyone during his lifetime. When he realizes that Lennie is slow-witted, he takes advantage of this weakness. Crooks urges Lennie to imagine a life of loneliness and despair, possibly to feel as though he [Crooks] isn't alone in his hopelessness. Students should discuss whether Crooks might be slightly insane, as indicated by his statements about being lonely to the point of sickness and his admission that he has hallucinations.)*
3. What does Crooks think about Lennie's dream farm? How does Candy's involvement with the farm affect this? *(Crooks thinks Lennie is wishing for something that will never happen. He claims men have come through the ranch with the same dream but says, "...nobody gets no land. It's just in their head" [p. 74]. When Candy adds that he has a plan for making money on the rabbits, Crooks admonishes him for taking part in Lennie's foolish dream. Candy insists that the dream is close to fruition, telling Crooks that they'll have the starting money soon. Upon hearing this, Crooks allows himself to hope that he might join the men on the farm, offering to work for room and board. For a brief moment, Crooks is optimistic about escaping his lonely life; however, the appearance of Curley's wife shatters Crooks' reverie.)*
4. What effect does Curley's wife have on Candy, Lennie, and Crooks when she enters the barn? What is her response to each of them? What is your opinion of Curley's wife? *(Candy is upset that Curley's wife has interrupted their talk about the dream farm. He is angry that she is always coming around and stirring up trouble for the workers. Candy admonishes Curley's wife for trying to entice the men and assures her that he is wise to her schemes. Crooks sits quietly at first, but he soon threatens Curley's wife so she will leave. Lennie just stands and stares at Curley's wife, not sure how to react to her entrance, her heavily made-up appearance, or the other men's treatment of her. Curley's wife scoffs at Candy's scolding, ultimately ignoring him to focus on Lennie. She responds to Crooks with racial slurs and threats of having him hung if he says anything to anyone. Answers will vary. Some students may feel that Curley's wife is a shameless flirt who delights in making the men uncomfortable and possibly even getting them into trouble by making Curley jealous. Other students may feel that Curley's wife is miserable and lonely at the ranch and is simply looking for companionship, albeit with the wrong people and using the wrong approach.)*

5. Before the men leave his room, Crooks calls out to Candy: "'Member what I said about [joining you at the farm]...I didn' mean it. Jus' foolin'. I wouldn' want to go no place like that" (p. 83). Analyze Crooks' change of heart. *(Answers will vary. Students should discuss Curley's wife's role in Crooks' change of heart, as well as his doubtfulness that he deserves anything good and his hopelessness that his circumstances will ever change.)*

6. What is Lennie's reaction to accidentally killing the puppy? Is Lennie upset about the loss of the puppy? How can you tell? *(As with everything that happens to him, Lennie is preoccupied with how the incident will affect his chances of tending the rabbits on his and George's dream farm. While Lennie understands that he killed the puppy, he is more concerned with George's punishment than the actual death of the puppy. He becomes angry and faults the puppy for dying, saying "Why do you got to get killed? You ain't so little as mice...Now I won't get to tend the rabbits" [p. 85]. Answers will vary. Students should discuss whether Lennie understands the finality of death and whether he is capable of comprehending the consequences of killing the puppy apart from how he is personally affected.)*

7. Recount the circumstances surrounding the death of Curley's wife. Do you believe Lennie is responsible for his actions? Defend your response. *(As Lennie contemplates the puppy's death, Curley's wife enters the barn. Lennie tries to ignore her, but she insists that he can talk to her freely. When Lennie reveals that he likes to touch soft things, Curley's wife offers him her hair. As Lennie strokes her hair more forcefully, she becomes angry and yells at him to let go. Lennie becomes frightened and holds on tighter, covering her face to stifle her screams and eventually shaking her so hard that he breaks her neck. Answers will vary; allow students to defend their positions. Students who believe Lennie is responsible for his actions might say that Lennie knew to avoid Curley's wife at all costs, with George making this very clear on multiple occasions. He also should have remembered what happened the other times he tried to "pet nice things" [p. 90]. Even though Lennie has the mind of a child, he should have released Curley's wife when she told him to. Students who don't believe Lennie is responsible for his actions may point out that Lennie was enticed by Curley's wife to touch her hair and his love for soft things overrode his instructions from George. Due to Lennie's mental state, he cannot be expected to remember the consequences of his previous actions, as he has difficulty processing situations. Because Curley's wife shouted at him, he panicked and clung to her instead of releasing her.)*

8. After Candy discovers Curley's wife's body, whom does he alert first? What plan is devised? What is Candy's primary concern? What is George's primary concern? *(Candy shows George the body first. George is saddened [although not very shocked] and worried about Lennie's fate at the hands of Curley and the other workers. George asks Candy to let him slip away to the bunkhouse for a moment because "the guys might think [he] was in on it" [p. 95]. After Candy tells the other men about Curley's wife, George will appear and act just as surprised as the others. Candy's primary concern is the dream farm. He seeks George's reassurance, but he knows from George's lack of response that the dream is gone. George's primary concern is Lennie's safety and whether Curley will hurt him if he finds him. He tries to reassure himself that Lennie will simply be put in jail, but he seems to know that Lennie won't get off that easy.)*

9. What do you think about George and Candy's plan? What might George's intentions be? *(Answers will vary. Students should discuss whether George actually intends to turn Lennie over to the men on the ranch, and if not, what the alternative is.)*

10. What does Lennie "discuss" with his aunt and the giant rabbit? What might this reveal about Lennie? *(Lennie starts assuring himself that he didn't forget where George told him to hide. He hears his aunt's voice scolding him for getting into trouble again and reminding him that he is a burden on George, who would do anything for him. Lennie also envisions a giant rabbit taunting him, "You ain't fit to lick the boots of no rabbit" [p. 102], essentially saying Lennie isn't good enough to tend the rabbits at the dream farm. The rabbit also says George will either abandon him or beat him. Answers will vary. Both Lennie's Aunt Clara and the giant rabbit represent his subconscious. Lennie may actually realize how much George has sacrificed for him over the years, and he feels guilty for this. He doesn't feel as if he deserves George's friendship, even though he craves it. He also fears that he is too clumsy and ignorant to do anything useful, believing instead that he should be punished for his bad behavior.)*

11. What do Lennie and George discuss in their hiding place? Why do you think Lennie insists that George scold him or banish him to a cave for killing Curley's wife? *(Lennie asks George to remind him how easy life would be without Lennie. George does so, in a somber monotone. Lennie also asks George to repeat the story about their dream farm, and George once again obliges. Answers will vary, but students should note that Lennie is terrified and wants to feel a sense of normalcy. By reenacting familiar conversations with George, Lennie can forget about what he's done and pretend that everything is alright. Lennie finds comfort in George's words, and he knows that any change in George's demeanor is a sign of trouble.)*

12. What does George do to Lennie as he recites the story about their dream farm? Why do you think he does this, and how do you feel about his decision? *(As Lennie relaxes and becomes lost in the story of the farm, George shoots Lennie in the back of the head with Carlson's gun. Answers will vary. Discussion should cover George's love for Lennie, his insistence that Lennie never be mistreated, his feelings of responsibility for Lennie's well-being, and his determination that Curley and the other workers not find and harm Lennie. While killing Lennie is technically murder, students should discuss George's motivations. Teachers should monitor this discussion closely, as opposing beliefs and values are likely to surface among students.)*

13. Analyze Slim's attempts at comforting George after the men come upon Lennie's body: "Never you mind...A guy got to sometimes...You hadda, George. I swear you hadda" (p. 107). *(Answers will vary, but students should note that Slim knows exactly what George has done, as well as his reasons for doing it.)*

Supplementary Activities

1. Write a eulogy for Lennie.
2. Complete the Qualities of a Hero activity on page 24 of this guide.

Post-reading Discussion Questions

1. Describe Crooks, Candy, and Lennie. What traits do they share, and why might people with these traits be attracted to the idea of joining George on the dream farm? *(Answers will vary, but as Curley's wife points out one night when talking with Candy, Crooks, and Lennie, the ranch workers "left all the weak ones [behind]" [p. 77] when they went into town. Crooks is an African American, and for that reason alone most others look down on him and exclude him from certain areas and activities on the ranch. He also has physical ailments such as his crooked back, which is probably where he gets his name. Candy is crippled [his missing hand] and is getting too old to work, so he does the small, undesirable jobs on the ranch. The others often ignore him because they deem him useless and weak. Lennie is looked down upon because of his childlike mind and is also feared because of his size and strength; most people are very wary of him. Because Crooks, Candy, and Lennie feel like outcasts and wish to be acknowledged [although Lennie doesn't necessarily recognize such feelings in himself], they are drawn to the idea of owning their own land where no one can condemn them, mock them, tease them, or dictate their actions. They seek freedom, self-governance, and a peaceful existence.)*

2. Why do you think George and Lennie share such a strong bond? *(Answers will vary. The two men have a long history with each other. George promised Lennie's aunt that he would take care of Lennie, and unlike most people, George understands Lennie's behavior. George protects Lennie at all costs, and although he grumbles about his responsibility, he obviously loves Lennie. George doesn't allow others to take advantage of Lennie's childlike mind. Lennie depends on George's stories of a better life and even his complaints about caring for Lennie. Whenever Lennie is confused or scared, he thinks of what George would do in order to determine his own course of action. The two men are each outcasts in their own way, and they love each other.)*

3. Is George a good friend to Lennie? Why or why not? *(Answers will vary. Some students may believe that George is a good friend because he promises Lennie's aunt that he will look out for him and has on many occasions put himself in harm's way to protect Lennie. Even though he knows his life would be much easier without Lennie, George refuses to abandon him. George constantly advises Lennie on how to stay out of trouble. He tells Lennie that he hopes they can "get a little stake together" [p. 30] in order to buy a farm and live in peace. In the end, George kills Lennie, knowing what consequences would await Lennie if he were caught by Curley and the other men. [This may be a point of contention among students. Use this discussion to explore students' differing opinions regarding the circumstances of Lennie's death.] Other students may point out that George has often been very cruel to Lennie. George admits that he "used to play jokes on 'im 'cause he was too dumb" [p. 40] and has beat him. George is insensitive to Lennie, and he often reminds Lennie how easy his life would be without him. Regarding Lennie's death, some students may feel that Lennie and George could have escaped the ranch together if George tried and that George killed Lennie because he was tired of sharing blame for Lennie's mistakes.)*

4. Which characters in the novel are static figures, and which are dynamic figures? *(Answers will vary. George is possibly the only true dynamic figure in the novel. In the beginning, he is snappy and mean-spirited to Lennie and constantly talks about how life would be wonderful without Lennie, even though he obviously cares for Lennie. He tells Slim that he used to treat Lennie terribly but that he changed, so his "dynamic" evolution started before the story began. By the end, George is deeply sympathetic toward Lennie's plight and seems depressed at the idea of killing him, but he does so in order to prevent any further harm to Lennie. Candy changes some throughout the novel, feeling first like an unappreciated old man and then becoming someone who has a dream. He is more forthright and assertive because of it and has something to look forward to for the first time in years. However, it is possible that after Lennie's death Candy reverts to his old ways. Most of the other characters remain static through the story. Slim remains quietly powerful, Carlson remains blusterous, Crooks remains bitter, and Curley remains angry.)*

5. In the novel, Slim is called "the prince of the ranch" (p. 33) and is described as a strong and fair leader. Do you agree with this assertion? Why or why not? *(Answers will vary. Most students will likely feel this is true, citing how calm, honest, and accepting he is with George and Lennie. He defends Lennie after Lennie crushes Curley's hand, forcing Curley to keep silent about the fight so that nothing terrible happens to Lennie. Slim comforts George after Lennie's death and seems to be the only one who understands what happened. He is widely respected, and every other ranch worker accepts his word as final. However, there is some evidence that he is a reluctant leader and not as strong-willed as many would assume. He does little to stop Carlson from shooting Candy's dog, instead telling Candy that he can have "any one of them pups [he] wants" [p. 48], basically trying to appease Candy rather than give a firm opinion on the matter. He also doesn't attempt to stop Curley from forming a murderous posse after finding his wife dead in the barn.)*
6. What do you think might have happened if George had decided to run away with Lennie instead of killing him? *(Answers will vary. Students should discuss how far the two men could have gotten once Curley reported the murder.)*
7. Why do you think the author included the scene concerning the death of Candy's dog? What might this have foreshadowed? *(Answers will vary, but the situation is a commentary on society. The dog was a faithful servant but had become old and burdensome—much like Candy, Crooks, or even Lennie. People in modern society have a tendency to rid themselves of things that grow old and obsolete. By killing the dog, the men rid themselves of an inconvenience, just as Candy fears he will be fired from the ranch once he becomes useless. The scene highlights that fear and also foreshadows Lennie's death, since both are considered "mercy killings" by the characters who cause the deaths.)*
8. Discuss the significance of Candy's statement: "I oughtta of shot that dog myself, George. I shouldn't oughtta of let no stranger shoot my dog" (p. 61). *(Answers will vary. Students should discuss how this relates to George killing Lennie and whether he might have gotten the idea from Candy.)*
9. Do you think there is an obvious villain in this novel? Why or why not? Regardless of your opinion, which characters can be classified as villains, and why? *(Answers will vary. Examples of villains include: Curley [antagonizes Lennie, instigates fights with others, uses his position as the boss' son to intimidate and threaten the ranch workers], Curley's wife [flirts with the ranch workers, acts inappropriately in her husband's absence, uses racial slurs when speaking to Crooks], Carlson [seems to enjoy confrontation, is insensitive to Candy, kills Candy's dog], and George [murders Lennie].)*
10. What was the most shocking scene in the novel, and why? *(Answers will vary. Some students may refer to the final scene in which George shoots Lennie. The act is shocking because the reader knows the bond between them is strong and the idea of killing a loved one [even to protect them] is unfathomable. Other scenes might include Lennie accidentally killing Curley's wife, Lennie crushing Curley's hand, and Carlson shooting Candy's dog.)*
11. Who was your favorite character in the novel, and why? In what ways could you relate to this character? *(Answers will vary.)*

Post-reading Extension Activities

Writing

1. Write a ten-line poem about a person or place from *Of Mice and Men*, omitting the name. Exchange poems with a classmate, and attempt to guess the identity of the person or place in the poem. For examples of poetic styles, ask your librarian or teacher for books of poetry to read and review.
2. In a two-page essay, write about your dream home and/or job. Compare and contrast your dream with the farm Lennie and George wish for, citing at least two differences and two similarities.

Reading

3. Read a professional book review of *Of Mice and Men* (you can find many online), and write a one-page response either agreeing or disagreeing with the critic. Support your opinion with evidence from the novel.
4. Read one of John Steinbeck's short stories, and explain at least three similar themes the story shares with *Of Mice and Men.*

Film/Drama

5. In groups of two or more, perform a scene from the novel for the class. Be sure to use costumes, props, and correct dialogue (omitting profanity) from the novel.
6. Watch the 1992 film version of *Of Mice and Men* (if necessary, obtain parental permission), and write a three-page analysis of the film comparing and contrasting it to the novel. Which do you think tells the story in a more effective way, and why?
7. Cast your own actors for a film version of *Of Mice and Men.* Use the character list in this guide as a basis. Choose an actor for each character, and in a paragraph for each, explain your choices.

Art

8. Examine the cover of *Of Mice and Men*, and create a new design idea based on a theme from the novel. Present your design to the class in a drawing, painting, or photograph (your own or found elsewhere). Be sure the design includes the title and author information, as well as a tagline or teaser for the cover.
9. Choose a character from the novel, and paint a picture or create a collage with images, symbols, and/or words that represent that character's importance in *Of Mice and Men.*
10. For each section of this guide, choose a symbol that represents the major action or tone of that section. Create a poster showing your symbols, and present your artwork in class.

Assessment for *Of Mice and Men*

Assessment is an ongoing process. The following ten items can be completed during the novel study. Once finished, the student and teacher will check the work. Points may be added to indicate the level of understanding.

Name ______________________________ Date ______________

Student	Teacher	
_______	_______	1. Write a one-page essay describing one favorable and one unfavorable trait of Slim, Candy, or Crooks.
_______	_______	2. Write two paragraphs explaining the origins and meaning of the title of the novel. Then, write two more paragraphs explaining why you think Steinbeck chose this title for the novel.
_______	_______	3. Using at least ten vocabulary words from the lists in this guide, write a two-page synopsis of *Of Mice and Men.*
_______	_______	4. Complete the Story Map on page 25 of this guide.
_______	_______	5. Write a one-page essay about one type of conflict in the novel, including whom it involves, how it develops, and how it is resolved.
_______	_______	6. Look online for an interview with John Steinbeck, and write a one-page essay discussing the interview.
_______	_______	7. Write an acrostic poem about a character or a theme from *Of Mice and Men* using one of the following: Steinbeck, loyalty, migrant, loneliness, Lennie Small, Curley's wife, or the title of the novel.
_______	_______	8. Write a one-page letter (of at least three paragraphs) to George after you have finished reading the novel. Include any advice, condolences, or questions you might have for him.
_______	_______	9. Write a recommendation for *Of Mice and Men* explaining what you liked and/or disliked about the novel.
_______	_______	10. Correct all quizzes taken over the course of reading the novel.

Attribute Webs

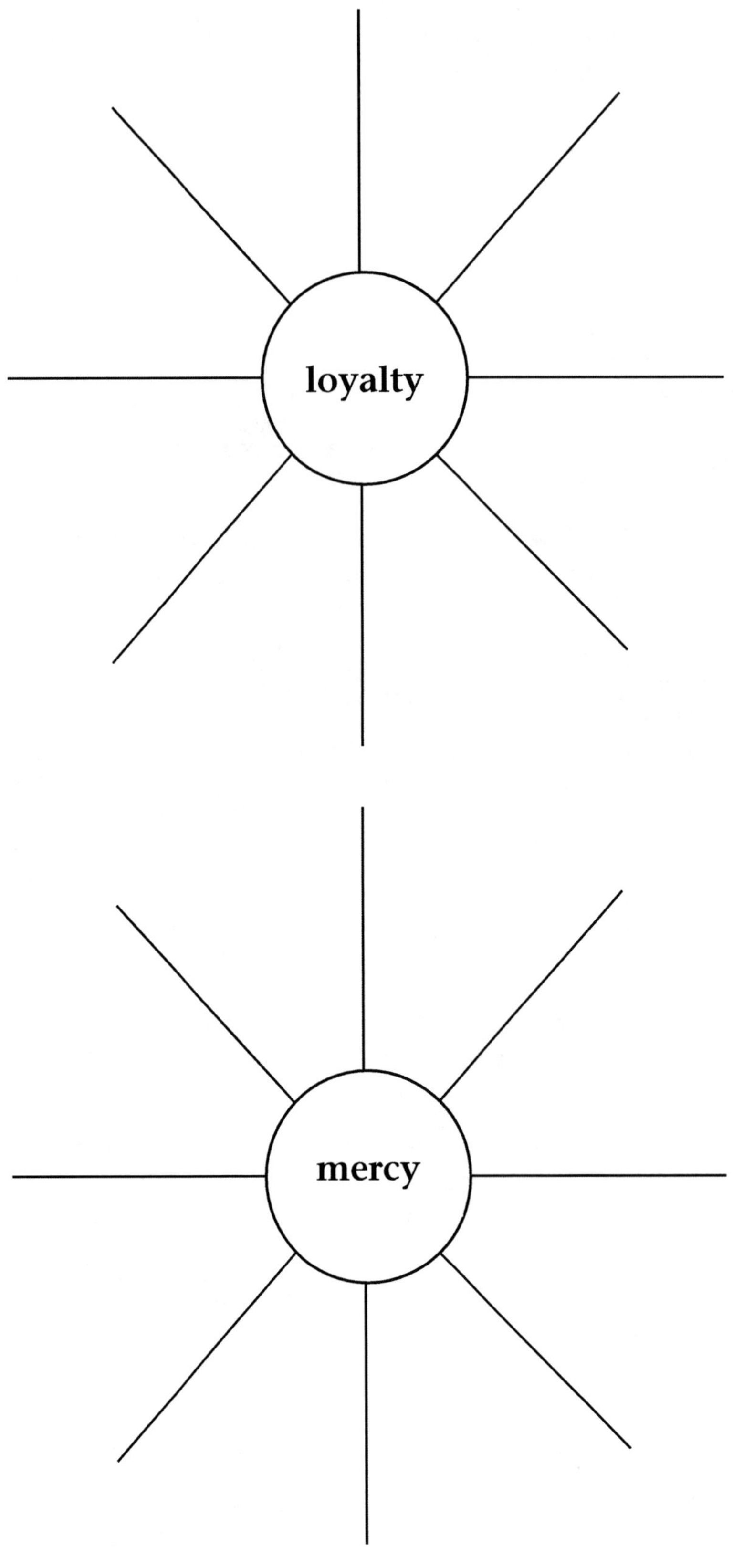

Vocabulary Word Map

Directions: Complete a word map for at least six vocabulary words from the first section of this guide.

Synonyms

____

____

____

Antonyms

____

____

____

WORD

____

Definition in your own words

____

____

____

Used in a sentence

____

____

____

Cause/Effect Chart

Directions: In the boxes below, explain the effects of George discussing the dream farm in front of Candy.

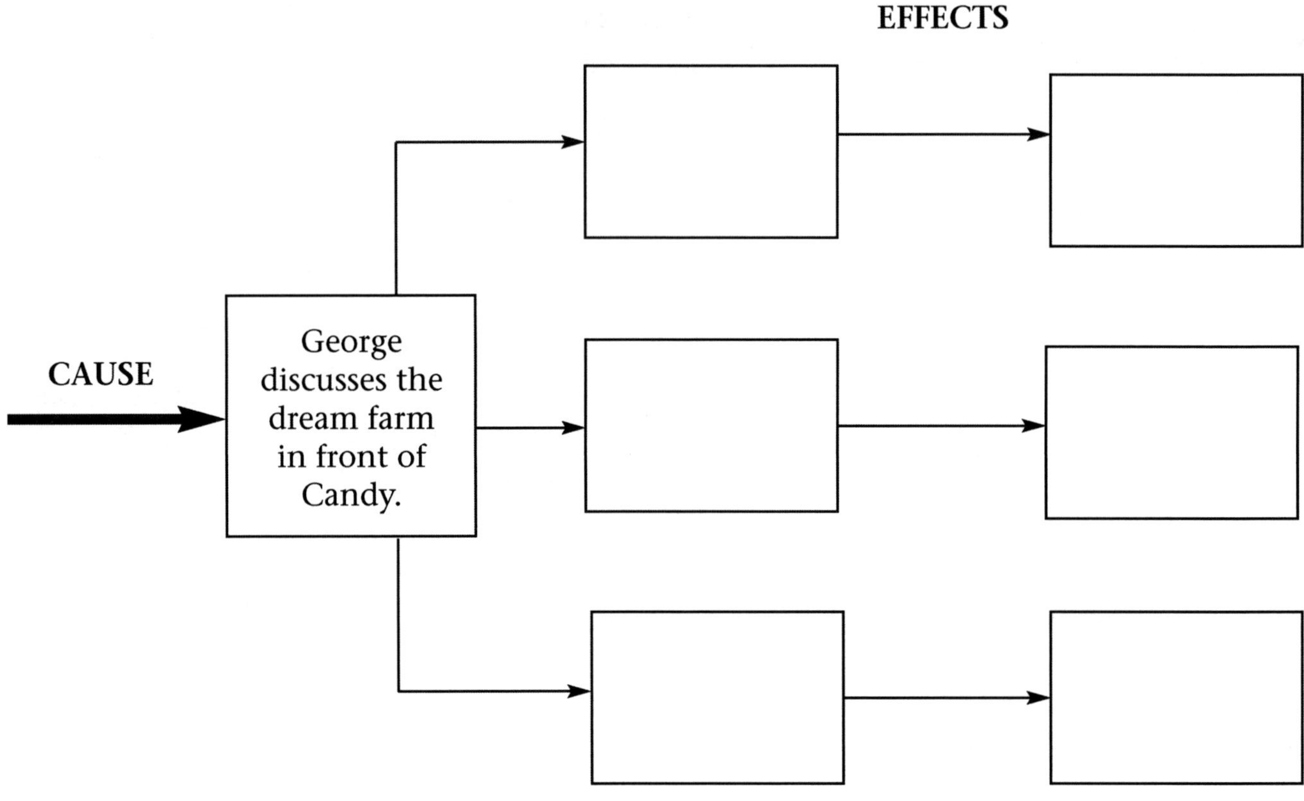

Thought Bubble

Directions: In the graphic below, write what George may have been thinking when Lennie crushed Curley's hand at George's command. Write from George's point of view.

Qualities of a Hero

Directions: Choose either George or Slim. For each quality listed in the left column, tell if the character has this quality. If you write "yes" in the second column, then you must list an event in the third column that proves that the character has the quality. If you write "no" in the second column, you may leave the third column blank.

Quality	Does the character have this quality? (yes or no)	Event from the Story
honest		
fair		
brave		
kind		
calm		
smart		
good friend		

Look at the chart you filled in above. Based on this information, do you think the character is a hero? Explain your decision on the lines below.

Story Map

Directions: Fill in each box below with information about the novel.

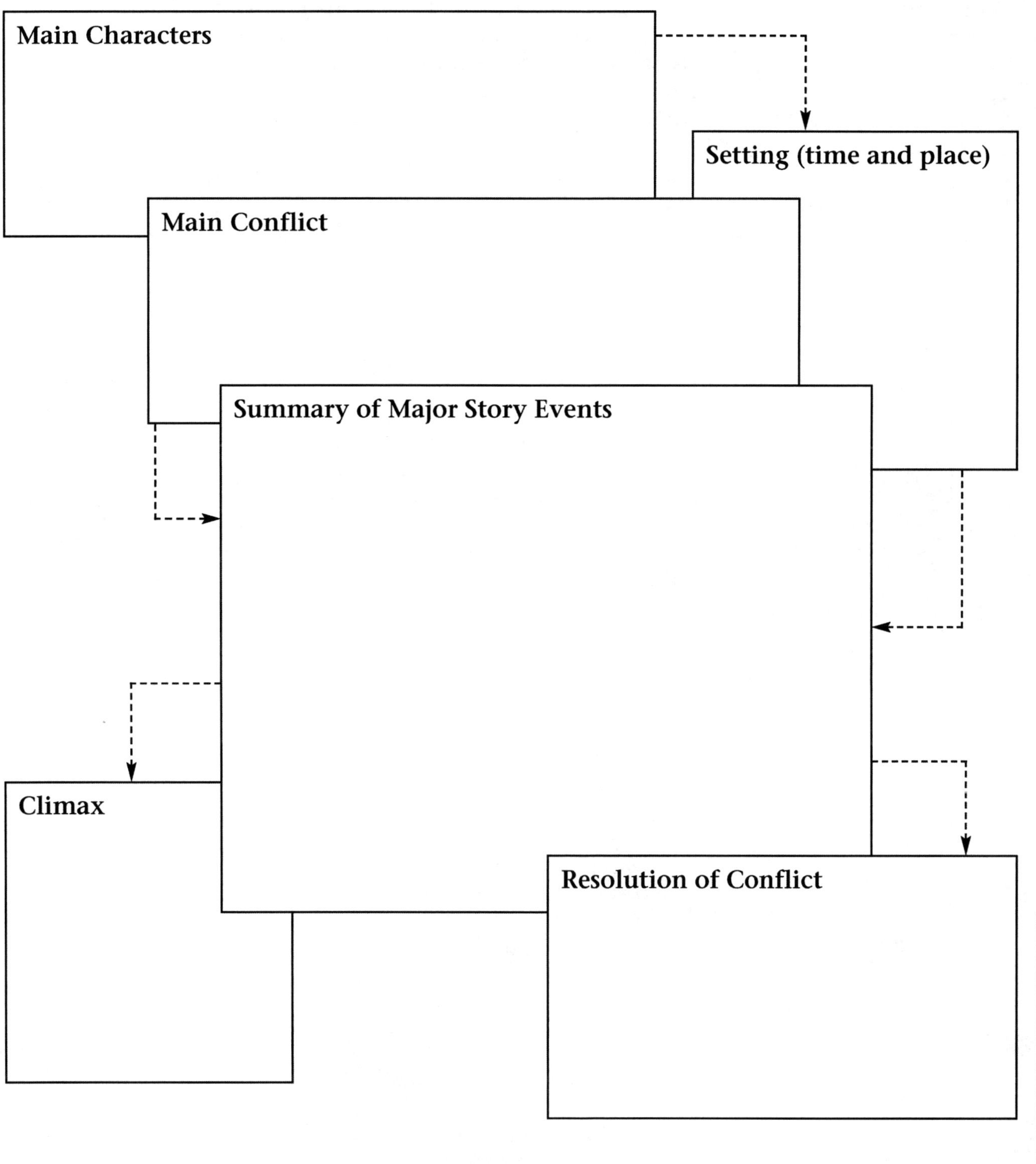

Linking Novel Units® Lessons to National and State Reading Assessments

During the past several years, an increasing number of students have faced some form of state-mandated competency testing in reading. Many states now administer state-developed assessments to measure the skills and knowledge emphasized in their particular reading curriculum. The discussion questions and post-reading questions in this Novel Units® Teacher Guide make excellent open-ended comprehension questions and may be used throughout the daily lessons as practice activities. The rubric below provides important information for evaluating responses to open-ended comprehension questions. Teachers may also use scoring rubrics provided for their own state's competency test.

Please note: The Novel Units® Student Packet contains optional open-ended questions in a format similar to many national and state reading assessments.

Scoring Rubric for Open-Ended Items

3-Exemplary	Thorough, complete ideas/information Clear organization throughout Logical reasoning/conclusions Thorough understanding of reading task Accurate, complete response
2-Sufficient	Many relevant ideas/pieces of information Clear organization throughout most of response Minor problems in logical reasoning/conclusions General understanding of reading task Generally accurate and complete response
1-Partially Sufficient	Minimally relevant ideas/information Obvious gaps in organization Obvious problems in logical reasoning/conclusions Minimal understanding of reading task Inaccuracies/incomplete response
0-Insufficient	Irrelevant ideas/information No coherent organization Major problems in logical reasoning/conclusions Little or no understanding of reading task Generally inaccurate/incomplete response

Glossary

Pages 1–37

1. recumbent: leaning; resting; lying down
2. bindle: bundle of clothing or bedding
3. brusquely: abruptly; harshly
4. elaborate: marked by complexity or fine detail
5. pantomime: conveyance through bodily or facial movements only
6. imperiously: dominantly; authoritatively
7. anguished: agonized; tormented
8. morosely: gloomily; sullenly
9. mollified: soothed in temper or disposition
10. pugnacious: having a quarrelsome or combative nature
11. derogatory: expressive of a low opinion
12. disengage: release or detach oneself
13. profound: having intellectual depth and insight

Pages 38–65

1. derision: use of ridicule or scorn
2. receptive: open and responsive
3. nuisance: something annoying, unpleasant, or obnoxious; pest
4. irrigation: supplying water to an area
5. cultivator: implement for loosening the soil while crops are growing
6. deliberate: slow, unhurried, and steady
7. sarcastically: spoken with intent to taunt or ridicule
8. subsided: became quiet; calmed down
9. reprehensible: worthy of or deserving disapproval or criticism
10. reverently: expressing respect or profound adoration
11. bemused: having one's attention fully occupied; absorbed
12. cowering: shrinking away from something (or someone) that menaces or dismays

Pages 66–107

1. accumulated: collected or gathered over time
2. liniment: liquid medicine applied to the skin, mostly to relieve pain
3. disarming: reducing or subduing criticism or hostility
4. apprehension: suspicion or fear, especially of a future evil
5. scornful: full of disdain or contempt, often mixed with anger at something perceived as unjust
6. crestfallen: ashamed; humiliated
7. sniveled: sniffed or snorted audibly; cried or whined with sharp, loud intakes of breath
8. skittered: scurried away lightly and quickly
9. retorted: made a reply; answered, usually sharply
10. belligerently: done in an assertive, hostile, or aggressive manner
11. monotonous: uttered or sounded in one unvarying tone

